DREAMLAND

PATTERN WRITING

Book - 4
Sentence Writing

DREAMLAND PUBLICATIONS
J-128, KIRTI NAGAR, NEW DELHI - 110 015, INDIA
Tel : +91-11-2510 6050, 2543 5657
E-mail: dreamland@dreamlandpublications.com
Shop online at www.dreamlandpublications.com
Follow us on www.instagram.com/dreamland.publications

I drink milk every day.

I drink milk every day.

I drink milk every day.

I drink milk every day.

He does his work every day.

He does his work every day.

He does his work every day.

He does his work every day.

A joker keeps us amused.

A joker keeps us amused.

A joker keeps us amused.

A joker keeps us amused.

Juice is very good for us.

Juice is very good for us.

Juice is very good for us.

Juice is very good for us.

My shoes are clean.

My shoes are clean.

My shoes are clean.

My shoes are clean.

A good boy helps others.

A good boy helps others.

A good boy helps others.

A good boy helps others.

A dog is a pet animal.

A dog is a pet animal.

A dog is a pet animal.

A dog is a pet animal.

I am working on the computer.

I am working on the computer.

I am working on the computer.

I am working on the computer.

  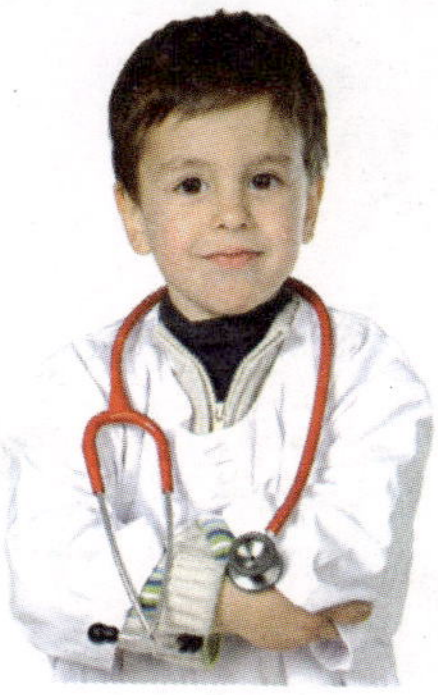

Work is worship .

Work is worship .

Work is worship .

Work is worship .

I have a red car.

I have a red car.

I have a red car.

I have a red car.

God is everywhere.

God is everywhere.

God is everywhere.

God is everywhere.

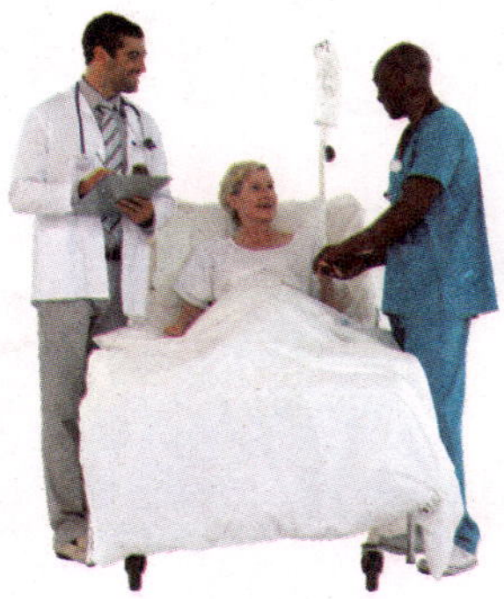  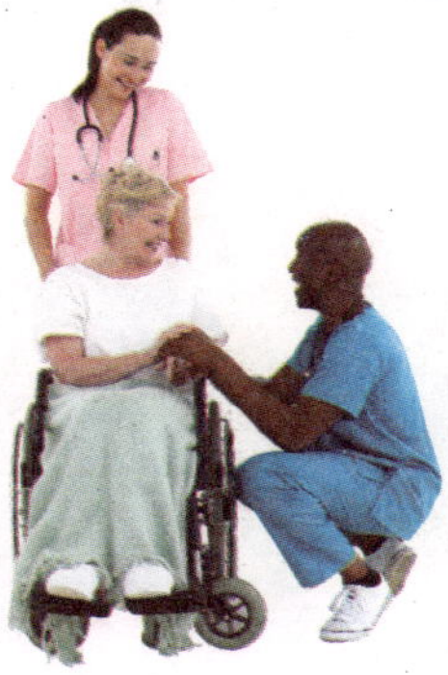

Do a kind deed every day.

Do a kind deed every day.

Do a kind deed every day.

Do a kind deed every day.

The sun rises in the east.

The sun rises in the east.

The sun rises in the east.

The sun rises in the east.

The lion is the king of the forest.

The lion is the king of the forest.

The lion is the king of the forest.

The lion is the king of the forest.

He lives in a cottage.

He lives in a cottage.

He lives in a cottage.

He lives in a cottage.

I like to eat mango .

I like to eat mango .

I like to eat mango .

I like to eat mango .

I go to school every day.

I go to school every day.

I go to school every day.

I go to school every day.

I write with a pen .

I write with a pen .

I write with a pen .

I write with a pen .

 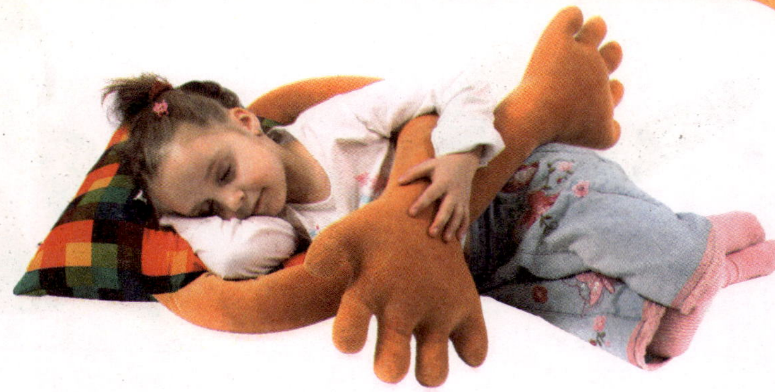

The child is sleeping .

The child is sleeping .

The child is sleeping .

The child is sleeping .

Roses smell very sweet.

Roses smell very sweet.

Roses smell very sweet.

Roses smell very sweet.

My house is very big .

My house is very big .

My house is very big .

My house is very big .

The moon shines at night.

The moon shines at night.

The moon shines at night.

The moon shines at night.

The stars twinkle at night.

The stars twinkle at night.

The stars twinkle at night.

The stars twinkle at night.

It is raining outdoors.

It is raining outdoors.

It is raining outdoors.

It is raining outdoors.

I like to read stories.

I like to read stories.

I like to read stories.

I like to read stories.

A fan gives us air.

A fan gives us air.

A fan gives us air.

A fan gives us air.

I am watching T.V.

I am watching T.V.

I am watching T.V.

I am watching T.V.

Bees give us honey.

Bees give us honey.

Bees give us honey.

Bees give us honey.

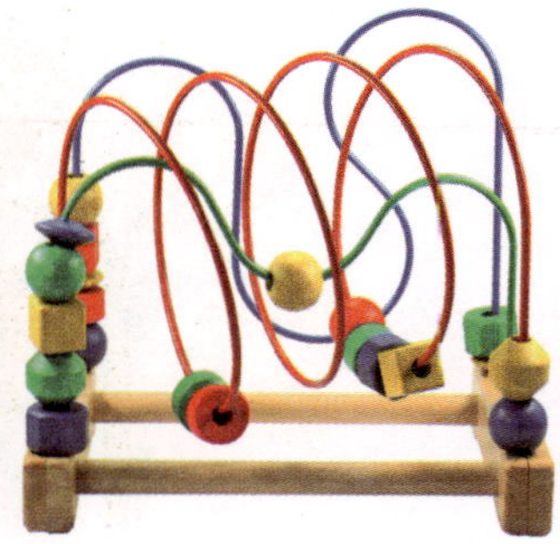

I have many toys.

I have many toys.

I have many toys.

I have many toys.

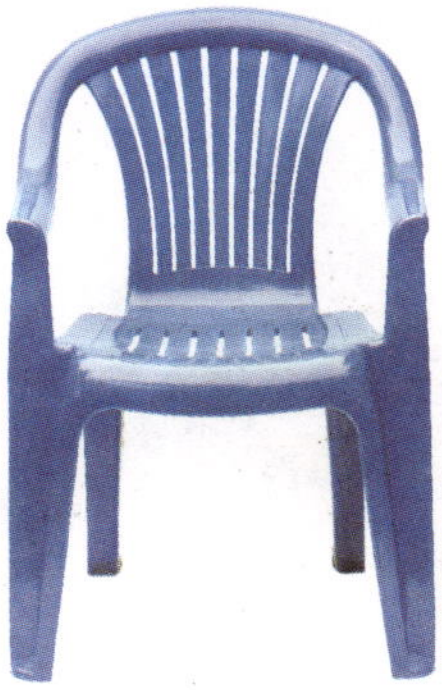  

A chair has four legs.

A chair has four legs.

A chair has four legs.

A chair has four legs.

Birds fly in the sky.

Birds fly in the sky.

Birds fly in the sky.

Birds fly in the sky.